Confidence
IN A MINUTE ▶▶

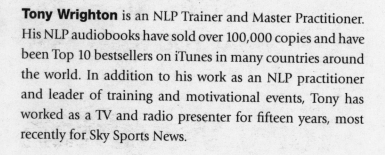

Tony Wrighton is an NLP Trainer and Master Practitioner. His NLP audiobooks have sold over 100,000 copies and have been Top 10 bestsellers on iTunes in many countries around the world. In addition to his work as an NLP practitioner and leader of training and motivational events, Tony has worked as a TV and radio presenter for fifteen years, most recently for Sky Sports News.

www.tonywrighton.com

Confidence
IN A MINUTE

10 STEPS TO GETTING
WHAT YOU WANT FAST

Tony Wrighton

2 4 6 8 10 9 7 5 3 1

Published in 2010 by Virgin Books, an imprint of Ebury Publishing
A Random House Group Company

The Random House Group Limited Reg. No. 954009

Addresses for companies within the Random House Group can be found at
www.randomhouse.co.uk

A CIP catalogue record for this book is available from the British Library

The Random House Group Limited supports The Forest Stewardship Council
[FSC], the leading international forest certification organisation. All our titles
that are printed on Greenpeace-approved FSC-certified paper carry the
FSC logo. Our paper procurement policy can be found at
www.rbooks.co.uk/environment

Mixed Sources
Product group from well-managed
forests and other controlled sources
www.fsc.org Cert no. TT-COC-2139
© 1996 Forest Stewardship Council

Printed in the UK by Bookmarque

ISBN 9780753522547

To buy books by your favourite authors and register for offers
visit www.rbooks.co.uk

Contents ▶▶

Introduction ▶▶

Each technique in this book takes a minute or less. That's all the time you need to start becoming more confident.

Don't believe the doom-and-gloom merchants who say you can't change, or that it'll take a lifetime of hard work to be more confident. They want you to fail. They want you to stay as you are, because it'll prove them right.

I used to listen to those people. It took me years of wanting more confidence before I actually did *anything*. When I finally took the first step, I wondered why I'd delayed it for so long.

Now, I'm here talking to you about it. But I'm not interested in being some sharp-suited self-help guru who makes you walk across hot coals. This is no ordinary 'self-improvement book' that takes itself too seriously. I'm just interested in helping you gain confidence quietly and quickly.

I've developed the techniques from my work as an NLP trainer and master practitioner, as well as the different things I've done over the last fifteen years working in TV and radio. NLP means Neuro Linguistic Programming and it pops up all over the place – sports, business, sales, marketing, therapy and many other fields. I learned from the best – the inspirational man who co-created NLP, Dr

Richard Bandler. And I've now discovered that people everywhere are really keen to get involved in basic personal development techniques that they can do straight away.

The focus of each chapter is on making sure that you actually take action towards *feeling* confident and *projecting* confidence. Many people have found the techniques I recommend to be effective. But I should issue a quick warning . . . I'm not looking to create 'confident idiots'. Don't start giving it the 'Tony Soprano'. Nobody likes an arrogant or over-assertive person who's so obviously trying to be a certain way. However much inner confidence you gain from this book – and it'll hopefully be loads – you are still you. Just a more confident you. The idea is to make you *feel* more confident, and once you feel that confidence, you might ask yourself how you can use it to make the people around you feel better as well as yourself.

As you go, if something works, feel free to write it down in the special section in the final chapter – 'The future'. Then you won't forget it and you'll end up having a guide on how to be confident that is written partly in your own words.

When you appear and feel confident, it can help you in almost every area of your life. This is true for casual conversations, formal meetings, presentations, speeches, job interviews, dates, sporting contests, and in every area of communication. I hope you find this book helpful.

CHAPTER ONE

To-do list ▶▶

Nick had spent a long time wishing he was more confident without actually doing anything about it.

The problem was that he didn't really think 'self-help' books were his style. In fact he'd felt vaguely embarrassed when he'd once bought a book on confidence. His friend had said, 'Don't get involved with all that self-help nonsense. You know it doesn't work.'

He tried to follow the instructions in the book, but everything seemed to take so long. It took him two hours to read the first chapter and he hadn't even got to the first exercise, let alone started to feel more confident. Then he put the book down for a moment, got distracted by the TV, and when he eventually picked it up again he was lost. It was just so wordy. He'd wanted more confidence for years, but why couldn't he open the book at any chapter and get on with it? Why couldn't they make it super-easy to follow?

I know what it's like. It's easy to keep on talking about getting more confidence without actually making any changes. That's why the focus of this first chapter is to make sure that you *do something*. Each exercise in the book requires just one minute of action so in a few moments' time you'll be on your way.

So you can start getting more confident quickly, in this chapter I'm going to ask you to:

▶▶ *work out exactly what your confidence goals are*

▶▶ *write down your confidence 'to-do list'*

▶▶ *set your 'to-do list' password reminder'.*

What exactly do you want?

First, work out your confidence goals.

What exactly do you want more confidence for? Is it a date, a presentation, a meeting, talking to people or perhaps feeling more relaxed in a particular situation? Or something else?

The more specific and succinct you can make your goals the better they will be. For instance, if you want more confidence delivering presentations, think about what exactly is going to help. Would it be feeling calm beforehand? Or feeling more positive beforehand? Or feeling more in control during the presentation itself? Or more relaxed? Or more prepared? Or looking more confident? Or projecting more confidence?

HINTS

- Put your confidence goals in the present, as if you've already achieved it.

- Express your goals positively. For example, *'I stop getting really nervous during business presentations'* is a poorly expressed goal because it focuses on something negative. *'I present with confidence and a smile on my face'* is a well-described goal.

- Add to each goal the date you want to achieve it by. It might be in days, weeks, months, years or even decades.

- Have as many different goals as you like. Here are some good examples:

  I look more relaxed delivering presentations
  I feel more relaxed delivering presentations
  I am confident and calm when I'm making a sale
  I am more confident and positive in my interview
  I feel in control around my boss
  I am a confident sportsperson
  I am able to stay calm and be confident in a high-pressure situation
  I am more positive about life and confident that things will turn out OK
  I feel confident and calm about my exams coming up
  I am excited about the forthcoming big speech
  I am calm just before the big speech
  I enjoy dating
  I am still the same person I always was, just a more confident version.

You can have as many different confidence goals as you like, as long as each one is specific.

See page 5 for some hints on how to express each goal. As soon as you've worked out how to do this, move straight to your confidence to-do list.

Your confidence to-do list

I have a friend who's really good at writing to-do lists. She's been making to-do lists for ever. It works well for her. She writes to-do lists at work, to-do lists at home, to-do shopping lists, even to-do lists for what to pack when she goes on holiday. She has lists all over the place, and she invariably does whatever is written down.

One day, I was at her house, and she was moaning at me about her life – her boss was giving her hassle, she didn't have a boyfriend and she was always short of money. Moan, moan, moan. I made a suggestion. 'What if you were to make a to-do list for your life?' I said. 'Then you might be as driven to achieve the really big things like a new job as you are to go and buy that four-pack of loo roll that you've just written down.'

She looked at me a bit strangely. But she wrote a 'life to-do list' anyway, and to her surprise she actually started doing the stuff on it.

If you write to-do lists, you probably already know you're more likely to get it done if you write it down. But do you also write down the really important things in life that you want to achieve? Like getting more confidence, for example?

I used not to write any of my goals and dreams down. I thought, 'What's the point? My goal is in my head anyway.' But then I started looking into the work of persuasion expert Dr Robert Cialdini. He has investigated the power of a written commitment, and cites Israeli researchers who found that 92 per cent of people took further action on a commitment they'd written down, compared to little more than half of those who hadn't written anything down. I was interested. Then I heard stories about famous people like Bruce Lee and Jim Carrey achieving big goals that they'd written down, and even how famous sprinter Michael Johnson wrote his goals down on a piece of paper and then inserted it in his shoe.

So I started writing my goals down too. Over time I started to notice how much more regularly I was getting things done. Now I find it satisfying when I look back over the goals that I set myself weeks, months and years ago.

HINTS

- Write your goals on your confidence to-do list in this book for easy reference. (1 minute per goal)

- You might also want to get a small sticky notepad and write your to-do list on it. Then stick it on your desk/wall/mirror/fridge/somewhere you will see it often. Just like you would with a normal to-do list. (Having the notepad will also come in handy for Chapter 8.) (1 minute)

So do it now. The longer you wait, the more likely you are not to do it. Now is a good time. As with everything in this book, it only takes a minute.

Here is an example of a confidence to-do list, using positive goals:

Date: *(example)* 15/10/11
Confidence goal: *(example)* I feel confident when I make my presentation to the sales team and I look it too.

Date: *(example)* 12/06/13
Confidence goal: *(example)* I am relaxed and calm when I go on a date.

Date: *(example)* 1/1/12
Confidence goal: I am confident and positive when I meet new people.

Date:
Confidence goal:

Date:
Confidence goal:

Date:
Confidence goal:

Date:
Confidence goal:

Date:
Confidence goal:

Date:
Confidence goal:

Date:
Confidence goal:

Date:
Confidence goal:

Date:
Confidence goal:

By the way, Dr Gail Matthews, a researcher in California, investigated goal-setting a step further. Her study suggests that if you share your goals with a friend, and then send them weekly updates, you are 33 per cent more likely to achieve them. Cialdini agrees that commitments are even more effective when they are public.

This is great for some, but I appreciate that working towards more confidence is an issue that people don't necessarily want to make public. If you do want to share, you might find a short weekly email to somebody you trust is manageable and helps you to stay committed to your goal.

Daily reminders

If you're going to become more confident, you want daily positive suggestions and reminders of where you're going. Because sometimes life takes over and we're simply so busy we start to get distracted.

Ever heard of a nineteenth-century French professor called Emile Coué? Nor had I, until I started investigating the idea he came up with called *affirmations*. It's said he cured hundreds of patients in Europe and North America by teaching them to repeat the following each morning and evening for hours at a time:

'Every day, in every way, I'm getting better and better.'

Now this approach may well have worked in the nineteenth century. But it probably wouldn't be appropriate today to walk down the street chanting, 'Every day, in every way, I'm getting better and better', so I decided to try and use the idea alongside modern technology. At first, I had people trying loads of different methods of setting their affirmation – email, social networking, alarms on the phone, even subliminal messaging programs on the computer. But I found the best answer was really simple, and something that you probably use every day anyway. Your email password.

Most of us 'log in' to something every day, so at a conscious level we have to ask ourselves – 'What is my password?' So now, using this technique, whenever you log in, you are remembering your goal at the same time. Of course, after a while, the process of remembering your password becomes almost automatic. Great. That means the process of remembering your goal also becomes automatic, and unconscious.

I recently told someone about this and she started laughing. 'What are you laughing at?' I asked her. 'Well, I've not had much luck with men over the past couple of years, so my password is allmenareevil.' No wonder.

So, what's your password going to be? Clearly it needs to be really short and sweet, so pick the goal that's most important and work out how to articulate that in just a few letters. (Even the process of thinking this out will help you to get closer to your goal.) Soon you will find that it becomes second nature to think about your password and your goal at the same time.

You can get creative. It's whatever works for you. Here are some examples of passwords other people have used – Confidence1, MoreConfidentAlready, strong7, meconfident, newconfidence2010, enjoydating, GettinBetter123, great-presentations, calmandconfident01, Ifeelgood. My favourite one was the tech support guy who wanted to feel more positive when he logged in at work every morning. He logged in with ComputerSaysYes.

▶▶ *Come up with whatever password you like that reflects your goal. Change your password now.* (1 minute)

▶▶ *Start to notice how it becomes second nature to think about being more confident whenever you log in.*

By the way, my password for the past couple of months has been TopConfBook. Although now I've announced it to the world I suppose I'd better go and change it.

The focus of this chapter is to make sure that you actually *do something*. If you're reading this and you haven't already written out your goals and set your password, go back. Do it now. Shoo! It only takes a minute. Only come back here when you're done.

When I met Nick, he'd wanted to change for a while but not done much about it. I talked him through the exact process we've just been through, of writing out his confidence 'to-do list' and then setting his password reminder.

He wrote out his confidence goals as if they were already happening. They looked like this:

I am more confident around John (his boss)
I feel confident in job interviews
Thailand will be great – it'll be the trip of a lifetime
I feel calm and relaxed on dates.

He dated each goal with the date by which he wanted to achieve it.

He then came up with his password reminder so he'd be reminded of his goals every day when he got to work. He started logging in with NickConfident. He'd finally started doing something about it.

TO-DO LIST – REMINDERS

▶▶ **Work out what you want. Be very specific about your confidence goals. Exactly when will you use this new confidence, and how? This will help you in the later chapters, and the rest of your life.** (1 minute)

▶▶ **Write out your confidence to-do list. Research shows we're more likely to achieve stuff when we write it down.**
(1 minute per goal on your list)

▶▶ **Remind yourself of your goal every day. How do you articulate your confidence goal in just a few letters? Set it as your email password** (1 minute to set up. Works whenever you log in)

CHAPTER TWO

Visualise it ▶▶

Sara's boss was a bully. He was intimidating, impatient and unpredictable. He never complimented her on her work, but was always very quick to criticise. He was an angry man and took out his stress on others. She started to make simple mistakes in his presence that she would never normally make.

The biggest problem for Sara was the important weekly presentation she had to make at the Monday morning meeting. Nobody ever knew what kind of mood the boss would be in. Sometimes he'd be all smiles if he'd had a good weekend or if his football team had won. But sometimes he'd be in a foul mood, telling people off and humiliating them in front of their co-workers. Once he'd even thrown a pen at somebody in anger.

Sara would spend her entire weekend worrying about the Monday morning meeting. She'd sit there, and think of all the ways it might go wrong. She'd see herself messing up, and imagine all the things she might say

and do that would incur her boss's wrath.

Consequently, her performance on Monday mornings got worse and worse, until even other co-workers were commenting on it.

Often, when we're nervous or lacking in confidence, we make pictures in our minds that aren't very helpful. This is a problem, because those negative pictures can act as a kind of script that the brain then follows. So in a situation like Sara's it becomes a vicious circle. Sometimes, the worse things get, the worse you imagine things will be.

The good news is that situations like this are not impossible to deal with. By using the technique of visualisation, you can start to change the way your brain thinks about future events and *feel* far more confident.

First, you can alter the unhelpful pictures to make them less powerful. Then you can make lots of really vivid, bright, positive pictures to replace them with.

Sometimes when I talk to people about visualisation, they think it's a bit wacky. They think they're going to have to put on a tapestry waistcoat, light a joss stick and sit in a dark room.

Well, I tell them this technique is the reason for many massive changes I've seen in people, as well as being the basis for inspiration in many different fields such as sport, art and business. Best of all, you can do it almost anywhere.

And it's worked for me too. For the last few years I've been doing a dream job – presenting sport on TV. After years of working on small local radio stations, when the TV role was advertised, I was desperate to get it. I wanted that job so badly.

But when I turned up on the day of the audition, I realised I wasn't the only one desperate for the job. There were no less than sixty eager and well-manicured hopefuls who'd turned up that day. So how was I able to give the audition that impressed the most? Visualisation.

Every day for two weeks beforehand, I saw myself sitting in the studio with everything going perfectly. I played the whole thing through on a big 3D cinema screen in my mind. I made the colours really bright and vivid, the sounds loud and clear, and I made it feel good. I heard myself saying the right things, and saw myself looking calm and confident. If doubts crept in, I would go back and run it again to see it go the way I wanted it to. Then I actually put myself in the picture. I imagined I was there, surrounded by it and feeling confident.

When I arrived on the day, it was a strange feeling because I felt like I'd done it before. Well I had – in my mind. I didn't feel quite so nervous and I knew exactly what to expect, because I'd seen it in my head so many times. I felt a quiet inner confidence.

Visualisation can help you to *seem* more confident, but its real power comes when it starts to help you *feel* more confident.

There are a number of different ways you can use visualisation to make changes:

▶▶ *how you see the old you*

▶▶ *how you see the new you*

▶▶ *how you see others.*

How you see the old you (or the dodgy telly technique)

Follow these steps to help change how you see the old you.

1 *Imagine you're looking at a really dodgy old TV. It was built in the 1980s, the reception is bad, the picture's a bit blurry and it has seen better days.*

2 *On this dodgy telly, imagine watching yourself at a time in the past when you've not been confident.*

3 *Make the picture grainy and blurred.*

4 *Make the picture black and white.*

5 *Move the whole TV away from you so the picture gets smaller.*

6 *Now pause the picture (i.e. make it still).*

7 *Continue trying to see this small, black and white, grainy image of yourself.*

The focus here is on creating emotional distance between that experience and now. That's why the dodgy telly has such a grainy picture. If you find this emotionally tough, then pause the dodgy telly. Push it further away – 50 metres away. Shrink the screen until it becomes tiny. Then switch it off, and move on to the 3D film technique.

How you see the new you (or the 3D film technique)

This technique will help you change how you see the new you.

1 *Imagine you're at the cinema in front of a huge 3D screen. You are watching a 3D film of your new confident self in a particular situation.*

2 *The 3D pictures are all around you, jumping out at you and surrounding you. The colours are really bright, and the images really sharp. Everything looks and feels great.*

3 *See yourself acting with the confidence you'd love.*

4 *Make yourself awesome. How good does it feel?*

5 *Make those colours even brighter and more vivid, the 3D images sharper, and at the same time, turn the volume up, and make it all feel more intensely positive. Enjoy it. Really treat yourself. (1 minute)*

That's the first part:

1 *Now imagine yourself floating into the film, and be completely surrounded by the 3D images. Run the film once again.*

2 *Really associate with the experience of being in the 3D film.*

3 *Take care to notice how great it feels when you start to act more confidently and things go exactly as you want them to.* (1 minute)

How you see others

For dealing with somebody intimidating (like Sara's boss) or a situation that leaves you feeling threatened, you might visualise a bit differently. Because by changing the way you think about them, you can change the way you react around them. The secret is to focus on removing power from the person.

1 *Make the intimidating person ridiculous in your mind. For instance, imagine seeing them belching, farting, picking their nose, naked, dancing, whatever seems out of place and makes you laugh.*

2 *You might also want to play around with their size. Make them very small; imagine them as a toddler waddling around in a nappy. Do whatever works for you. Have fun with it.*

3 *Make the images big in your mind. See and hear exactly how the new version of the person appears to you, and notice how differently you feel about them now.*

4 *Make sure you stick with this exercise for the full minute every time.* (1 minute)

This might sound silly, but the connections that the mind forms are very powerful. By practising this technique you are starting to change the way your brain perceives these difficult people at a deep level.

Get the visualisation habit

The more you can use visualisation in the three specific ways I have described, the more you can get into the habit of regularly approaching a particular situation on your mind more positively.

A friend of mine once said, 'Tony, I can't visualise.' I asked him, 'What does your car look like? What colour is it? Describe it to me.' Strangely he could tell me in great detail as he pictured in his mind exactly what it looked like. If you can describe how your car (or anything you choose) looks, you can visualise.

When I met Sara, she was a nervous wreck. This was partly down to the fact that her boss was a bully, but also in part due to her making big powerful pictures in her head every weekend about how badly the Monday meeting was going to go. I said to her, 'You can't change your boss, but you can start to change the way you think about him.'

I got her to visualise the Monday meeting in a totally different way. In her head she saw herself standing there tall, proud, in control. She was organised and efficient. She saw herself standing very still. She took care in her visualisation to look at everybody in the room, talk slowly and confidently, and smile. She even imagined telling the odd joke, and she saw her workmates laughing along with

HINTS

■ You can use visualisation *almost anywhere*; on the train, in a comfy armchair, in the garden, first thing in the morning when you wake up. Don't do it driving or operating machinery. Do it when it's safe to drift off for a minute. Close your eyes or keep them open, whatever works. Take one minute daily and really get into it.

her. She imagined her boss to be ninety years old, a tiny little old man who wasn't powerful any more. She didn't want to be rude to him, just to be slightly more immune to his insults, so that when he did come up with one of his regular criticisms she was able to smile rather patronisingly at him and let it wash over her.

At first, Sara found this really hard. When she tried to imagine a patronising smile, all she could think of was how nervous she was in his presence. But over time, she started to get better at visualising a positive meeting. Then she started to get more confident. Her workmates began to comment on how calm and efficient she appeared on Monday mornings. She became much better at thinking about her work positively, and enjoyed her weekends more too.

What of her boss? Well he didn't really change at all, but Sara never expected him to. Because when you make the change yourself, you don't need to rely on others.

VISUALISE IT – REMINDERS

▶▶ Change the way you see your old self. Use the dodgy telly technique to reduce the impact of any bad memories. Follow the instructions closely. Remember to make it a rubbish old TV that barely works. Repeat until negative emotions start to be reduced. (1 minute each time)

▶▶ Change the way you see your new self. Visualise a huge 3D film of your new confident self. Shut your eyes if it helps. The more you can do this, the more you'll start to make lasting changes at a deep level. (1 minute)

▶▶ Change the way you see other people. When you are dealing with somebody intimidating, visualise them as ridiculous and take away their power. By doing this you can start to change the way you communicate with them. (1 minute)

▶▶ Use visualisation daily to get lasting confidence, first thing in the morning, on the train, at your desk, wherever is good for you. The more you do it, the better you get at it. (1 minute daily)

CHAPTER THREE

Deal with nerves ▶▶

Alex was preparing to go on yet another first date.

As she thought about the evening ahead – drink, meal, polite conversation – she felt a familiar tight knot in her stomach. She knew the feeling well. Not exactly pain. But a physical sensation. It felt like her stomach was all bunched up. It felt tight, contracted, nauseous even. And she knew when she felt that feeling, she became tense.

On her last date she'd felt terrible. She could hear her heart beating while she was talking to him. Her voice sounded different to normal. The nerves seemed to make her act in odd ways too. She'd made a harmless but slightly raunchy joke. He'd looked rather shocked, and departed after less than an hour, leaving her sitting there all alone with only a cold cappuccino for company.

So now these nerves made her feel awful and act differently. She needed to do something about it. She needed to regain control.

Nerves can be very debilitating. In the worst instance, they can affect somebody's entire approach to life. And everybody – absolutely everybody – gets them.

In this chapter you'll find some simple, effective techniques for *managing* nerves. Follow these six techniques, and you'll start to physically *feel* better and reduce the impact of those nerves:

▶▶ *Breathe*

▶▶ *Squeeze*

▶▶ *Move*

▶▶ *Disco Ball*

▶▶ *The Window*

▶▶ *The Best Moment of your Life*

The first three, Breathe, Squeeze and Move, all have a positive physical impact that can help change the way nerves feel. Disco Ball works by giving those nerves physical characteristics in your mind. The fifth exercise, The Window, looks at how you can permanently alter the way you think about a bad memory. The final one, The Best Moment of your Life, gets you thinking about the future in a different way.

You may be sceptical. You may have unsuccessfully tried lots of different methods to get rid of these nerves and be pretty doubtful about whether you can do anything about it. That's fine. Just read on. Read the rest of this section, and see what happens. I have used variations of some of these exercises in my audiobooks and many people have told me how useful they find them.

One more thing. When we say we have 'nerves' or are feeling 'nervous', we are actually experiencing the effects of extra adrenaline being pumped round the body in response to a perceived threat. This feeling can make you feel sick to the stomach, but it can also make you feel excited, switched on and sharp.

If you were to *totally* take that away, it would leave you without any adrenaline when you need it most. You want some adrenaline because it makes you more alert, feeling more alive and aware of the world around you. This is obviously handy in important situations. So part of this chapter looks at how to accept 'nerves' and how to start using them to your advantage.

So, how can we alter the physical impact of that adrenaline?

Breathe

I love yoga, even though I'm a typical bloke who can't touch his toes. Those ancient yogi in India were on to something when they said that breathing deeply can clear and cleanse the mind and body.

I've tried lots of relaxation and meditation techniques, and I believe some of the most effective are the breathing techniques in yoga. They have been in existence for up to 5,000 years, which is a pretty good endorsement in itself. Use the Breathe technique, where you find a spare minute to take some deep breaths in and out, to feel calmer:

1 *Really fill your lungs when you breathe in. Breathe in through the nose.*

2 *Make the exhalation twice as long as the inhalation. Breathe out slowly through the mouth. (In many yoga practices the exhalation is around twice the length of the inhalation to promote a sense of meditation and calm.)*

3 *Be aware that when you breathe in you're bringing extra oxygen in and turning nutrients into fuel.*

4 *When you breathe out, you are getting rid of all that stale air and carbon dioxide and the physical sensation of release relieves tension. Continue to exhale for twice as long as you inhale.*

5 *Do this for the full minute for maximum benefit.*
   (1 minute)

The ancient yogi said that 'breathing is the key to life'. When a person needs to relax, the yogi say that by concentrating on the breath, one can create a 'calm and serene state of being'.

By the way, if you ever walk past a yoga class and you see a very unbendy person wobbling around uncomfortably on one leg, that's me.

Squeeze

Use the Squeeze technique to physically relax your body. The more you practise it, the better the results you will get. I first came across it as a sports psychology exercise, and it is used by many sportsmen and women. It is very simple, quick and effective, and has its origins in progressive muscle relaxation (PMR), a technique developed more than seventy years ago, which involves tensing and releasing all the major muscle groups in the body. This is what you do:

1 *Clench both hands into tight fists. Go on, squeeze as hard as you can. Harder. Make them tense. See white knuckles. Hold for a few seconds.*

2 *Slowly release, and at the same time extend your arms and hands away from your body with your open hands facing upwards.*

3 *Allow yourself to notice how the muscles relax as the tension flows away. Really take care to notice all those feelings of relaxation spreading from your hands all the way through your body.*

4 *Repeat as needed. (1 minute)*

In this technique, you're taking all of the tension in your body and channelling it. It's like a much shorter and less violent version of a boxercise class.

If you like, you can combine Breathe and Squeeze. Breathe deeply in as you squeeze, and out as you release, remembering to exhale for twice as long as you inhale.

Move

I know from experience how hard it is when you're trying to tell your muscles to relax, and it's just not happening. That's why a number of these exercises are genuinely physical in nature. Not thinking, but doing. A number of actors I know use a version of this as they prepare for a show. Use the Move technique to alter your state and change your mood.

1 *Whatever you're doing, change your physical state. Move about, change location, stretch, shift your seating position, just make it different and, as you're doing that, think of a time when you felt radiant and happy and confident. It can be a small movement too. If you're in a meeting or an exam, then a stretch or a shift in seating position can have the same effect.*

2 *Notice how your altered physicality has helped shift your mental state.*

3 *That's it.*

4 *Yes, that really is it. But take care to notice any shift in your mental state. How could you use that shift in mood when you need it most?* (1 minute)

A research team at Georgia State University tested the importance of movement by depriving schoolchildren of a break between classes on certain days. They found that on the days the children were allowed a break (and therefore allowed to move around for a short while), they were consistently 'more on task and less fidgety' afterwards.

It's thought even quite small movements start to increase blood circulation and send oxygen to the brain, which help you to think more clearly and rationally. So take a break, move around, and notice how it changes your mood.

Disco Ball

Some people say their nerves feel like a physical churning in the stomach. Disco Ball works by giving nerves characteristics of colour and movement in your mind, and you can use this technique to change the way you *think* and *feel* about nerves.

This is adapted from NLP co-creator Dr Richard Bandler's excellent 'spinning' technique. I originally picked a disco ball because it reminded me of good times (and my bad dancing). Since then, many people have told me how effective they find it. This is what you need to do:

1 *Think about the nerves that you get.*

2 *Visualise the feeling as a coloured disco ball spinning inside you.*

3 *Give it an unpleasant sickly greeny-yellow colour. Notice which way it's spinning. It could be moving in any direction so take care to notice which way it's going.*

4 *Slow the sickly greeny-yellow ball down until it eventually comes to a halt.*

5 *Now give the disco ball your favourite colour. Give it beautiful lighting and brightness, and start to reverse the movement. The ball is now moving in the opposite direction.*

6 *Now make the movements of your disco ball faster. Spin it faster and faster as you look at it. Make it rocket-powered. The faster it spins, the better you'll start to feel. Make the glow of the lighting even more beautiful. As you spin your disco ball even quicker, the feeling of nervousness starts to become more comfortable.*

7 *Keep spinning the disco ball faster until you can acknowledge that the nerves are still there, but the unpleasant feeling is reduced and replaced by a calmer, more neutral feeling. (1 minute. Repeat whenever you like)*

Remember, nobody expects you to go from very nervous to super confident in one minute. It's about making small changes so you can start to feel more neutral about nerves.

HINT

- You can pick whichever colour you like for your disco ball. You might want to pick the deep blue of the sea when you last went on holiday, or a powder blue sky, or the colour of a beautiful sunset, or the colour that you've just painted your new living room. Anything goes – over the years people have come up with all sorts including fluorescent pink and the colour of a favourite football team. Just make it a colour that you really like.

The Window

Use The Window technique if you've had a particularly bad experience with nerves at some point in your past. It can be quite common to be held back by a bad memory and this technique can work very effectively to counter its effects.

The Window starts to make it easier for you to disassociate from the emotion surrounding the event.

1 *Imagine you are looking through a small glass window with a thick frame. Through this window you can see yourself. You are looking at a small handheld video screen, like an iPhone, propped up on a table. (It's you*

looking through a window, watching yourself, *watching the screen.)*

2   *Watch yourself watching the negative confidence experience in black and white. Make sure to start it at a time beforehand when you felt safe and relaxed. Watch it through in black and white. Finish it on pause at another time afterwards – any time at all – when, again, you felt safe and relaxed.*

3   *Imagine yourself on the other side of the window, and imagine yourself in the screen, so you are now in the picture, surrounded by that safe and relaxed moment you just paused.*

4   *Make your surroundings colour. Start to rewind, so that it rewinds in colour around you. Ensure that in a few seconds, you are paused back at the start again.*

If at any point this feels uncomfortable, step out of the picture again, return to your position behind the window and make the picture on the small screen lower quality, lower resolution, and harder to see clearly. Remember, you go forward in black and white, and backwards in colour.

1   *Now go back to behind the window and repeat this process, but this time make the black and white video on the screen more and more blurry. It's like something you've downloaded from YouTube and the quality of the file is so poor it's quite hard to follow what's going on.*

2 Repeat again, and make the glass in the window a little blurry and dirty, so it's slightly harder to see through. Mute the volume on the screen. (Remember, you are still behind the window, watching yourself watching the small screen.)

3 Repeat the above, making the window smaller. Keep repeating until you feel the negative emotions surrounding the event have become more neutral emotions. That's what you want. You don't have to look back and love the memory. You can just feel more neutral about it.

4 When you feel more neutral, go back behind the window, and watch yourself leave the small screen on the table, and walk away. (Each repetition – 1 minute)

The window puts a mental barrier between you and the event. The low-res video, general bad quality of the picture and size of the screen make it harder to associate with the negative emotions surrounding it. The colour rewind scrambles and confuses the way your brain thinks about the episode. You'll find the memories are still there but they don't hold the same power over you that they once did.

The Best Moment of your Life

This exercise is about something great in your life that hasn't happened yet, and its purpose is to change the way you think about nerves. First, remember that everybody gets them. I know a famous DJ who told me he gets such bad nerves he is sometimes sick before a gig. 'The weird thing,' he said, 'is that I need those nerves. Those nerves are what I call "good nerves". I couldn't function without them. They give me adrenaline and help me to get psyched up for the gig. They help me to know that I care about what's about to happen.'

His gaze got more intense.

'And when I think about it I've had this feeling before most of the best experiences in my life.'

Here's how to run the Best Moment of your Life technique:

1 *Think of the 'Best Moment of your Life' that hasn't happened yet. It might be a proposal, a wedding, a birth, a successful performance or achievement, winning the lottery, doing a dream job or watching your child achieve something special. Something important that you'd really care about.*

2 *Play it through in your mind as if it were to go perfectly. Hear what you'd hear, see what you'd see and notice how good this important moment in your life feels.*

3 *Pay particular attention to any adrenaline (nerves). Notice how it feels, and the important thing is to notice how they help you in this best moment of your life. (The adrenaline can help you to be more alert, more present, provide a state of readiness, give you a lot more energy and help you to appreciate the importance of the moment.)*

4 *Notice how great experiences and 'good nerves' might combine in a positive way. (1 minute)*

Remember, you're playing it through as if the episode goes perfectly. That is the point. Enjoy it – you are thinking about an amazing experience. Here's an example:

> Making a speech at my wedding. I am nervous, excited, tense, alert. I have lots of adrenaline pumping round my body. If I didn't – if I was totally relaxed – I wouldn't be alert enough to remember everything I need to, and be totally prepared and ready, and take in the whole experience too. If I was totally relaxed I might miss something. How could I possibly be completely relaxed right now? I need *some* adrenaline to appreciate that this is one of the best moments of my life. I need these 'good nerves'.

Often the most effective strategy of all is to remember that you're feeling these 'good nerves' because you want to succeed.

With these exercises, the best thing to do is give them all a go and find out which one works for you. Do what works.

I got Alex squeezing and focusing on her breathing before dates. Then she would spin her (pink) disco ball. These techniques couldn't change the suitability of the men she met, but she said she found practising them helpful, particularly in terms of the physical tension that she felt.

But she said, for her, the most effective strategy was remembering that she was feeling those nerves for a reason, because when she went on a date, it was important to her and she wanted it to go well. In other words, she started thinking of them as 'good nerves'. She vowed to use the strategy to get out there and find somebody great who would laugh at her slightly raunchy jokes.

DEAL WITH NERVES – REMINDERS

'Nerves' result from extra adrenaline travelling from the brain to the rest of the body. We can alter the physical impact of that adrenaline in different ways:

▶▶ **BREATHE.** Yoga breathing oxygenates the muscles and organs, resulting in a state of meditation and calm. Go twice as long on the out-breath. (1 minute)

▶▶ **SQUEEZE.** Channels and then releases any physical tension that you are carrying. (1 minute)

▶▶ **MOVE.** Altering your physical state can in turn alter your mental state. (1 minute)

▶▶ **DISCO BALL.** Imagine those nerves as a disco ball spinning inside you. By changing the colour and direction of your disco ball, you can change the way the brain feels about nerves. (1 minute)

▶▶ **THE WINDOW.** Use this technique to get over a serious past episode that prevents you from gaining confidence. Repeat until its emotional impact is reduced. (1 minute each repetition)

▶▶ **THE BEST MOMENT OF YOUR LIFE.** Think about something really good in your future. As you do the exercise, start to notice how adrenaline could be a positive thing for that event. (1 minute)

CHAPTER FOUR

How you look ►►

Nikki made quite big public presentations. And she wanted to confide in me.

'I don't feel all that confident you know. Sometimes, when I'm up there ready to go, I feel scared. Truly scared. I know that people have come to listen to me, but as I see them entering the room all I want to do is curl up into a little ball.'

'So what do you do?' I asked.

'At the start I subtly alter my body language, and that changes the way I feel. I walk out with purpose, as if I really was feeling confident. I hold my head up straight. I stand at the front and plant my feet firmly on the floor. I stay quite still at first, and that helps me to talk more slowly and feel more confident. I look people in the eye and smile. I use my arms to make a point and make sure they're uncrossed. I really just do it to make myself feel better. Knowing that I'm projecting a bit more confidence makes me feel in control. Of course I need to have a

good speech too, but the other stuff generally seems to come more naturally after that.'

Changing your body language can do two things.

▶▶ *It can alter the way you're* perceived. *We have preconceived ideas of how others are feeling based on how they look, whether they actually are feeling that way or not.*

▶▶ *It can alter the way you* feel. *By subtly altering your body language to project more confidence, you start to* feel *more confident too.*

I have learned from experience how subtle physical changes can alter the way a person feels. Being on TV is a situation that is clearly fairly unnatural. My instincts when I started out were deliberately to cross my arms in front of me in a protective way.

It looked defensive and I felt uncomfortable. I started to watch other presenters closely. They seemed naturally to sit upright, with their heads straight in a position that appeared to convey confidence and authority. Their arms were open, whereas I was still instinctively closing myself off. When I started applying what I'd observed, it felt better. First I projected more confidence, and then I started to feel it.

This chapter looks at the perceptions we have of body language and the opinions we form. It's great to work out how to use body language to appear more confident and communicate more successfully. But there is no absolute right or wrong, or concrete rules – just common interpretations of body language and what it means. For instance, somebody hanging their head down might be displaying a lack of confidence. However they might also just be very tired. So when reading other people's body language it is helpful to look for groups of signs at once.

The most important thing is to increase your body language self-awareness. The more you do that, the more you can control the way you feel and the signals you're giving out. Then you can start to *feel* more confident.

Be aware that perceptions of body language vary across cultures. My observations are based on traditional western interpretations of body language.

One more thing. Remember this. You are still you. Nobody likes an idiot. If you suddenly start giving it the Tony Soprano attitude then people will suss you out very quickly. Remember your values and beliefs, and communicate with confidence and respect.

Open arms, open body language

Arms crossed or folded are generally perceived as defensive and negative. Some people will tell you it feels comfortable, and it may well be. Others might say it's cold and they're doing it to warm themselves, which of course is fine, and something that most of us do from time to time.

However that doesn't change the *perceived* defensiveness of crossed arms. And that's the image you may be projecting. This crossing of arms is often interpreted as an unconscious barrier. In fact some body-language researchers liken it to self-hugging. They say when we were young and needed comforting our mothers would hug us. Now our mothers aren't always there so in times of stress some people do it to themselves.

When we uncross our arms, we are perceived to be more open and relaxed. If you really find it hard to remember not to cross them, hold a drink/pen/folder/anything else.

And this 'openness' doesn't just apply to the arms, it goes for the whole body too. Closed body language is perceived as representing the defensiveness you feel. Open body language = open attitude. Remember, these are just common perceptions, and the most important thing is to *feel* more confident. For example, many women prefer sitting with their legs crossed. A good way round this can be pointing those crossed legs towards whoever you are communicating with. This is perceived as projecting a more positive and confident image (see 'Feet and legs' for more).

Smile

Studies show that when we smile, we release 'feel-good chemicals' in our brain. These substances (if you want to get scientific – endogenous opioid polypeptide compounds) can make us feel euphoric, happy and calm, and can even relieve pain.

In one fascinating study by two researchers called Davis and Palladino, people were told to hold pencils in their mouths. Some held the pencil with their teeth (to encourage a smile). Others were told to hold the pencil in their mouth without using their teeth (so unable to smile). Then they all watched cartoons. Afterwards, the ones holding the pencil with their teeth (and therefore able to smile) rated the cartoons as funnier.

As well as making you *feel* good, smiling also *projects* a relaxed and confident image. This is because body language is a reflection of your level of confidence, and smiling portrays happiness and an inner ease. And research shows the more we smile, the more positively people will react to you, which will help you feel more confident.

Head up straight

Holding your head up straight helps you to appear positive and confident. Along with moving the chin out (see page 46), you can use this technique to make yourself look and, more importantly, feel more confident.

By contrast, head down tends to signal low confidence, introspection and self-doubt. Think of a footballer who's just missed a penalty, trudging back to the half-way line with his head bowed.

A head tilt is perceived as interested and friendly, but can also indicate submission and a lack of confidence. Body-language expert Patti Wood says head tilt mimics a movement done by wolves to the leader of their pack. She says it symbolises the baring of the neck to a superior, saying, 'I'm exposing my most vulnerable spot to you to show you I know you can rip me to pieces. So let's not fight about it.'

Chin out

As the head moves up obviously the chin moves out, and there is a fine line here between perceived confidence and aggression.

Thrusting the chin out is an aggressive sign. It might be useful on some occasions when you feel intimidated by somebody or when you want to impose yourself on somebody, like a sporting situation. The chin thrust can project confidence, and also arrogance. If you try it, how does it make you feel? Likewise, chin down is perceived as a defensive sign and even protecting the vulnerable neck area.

As with all these body-language postures, be careful with the chin thrust. Do you want to be perceived as confident or aggressive? Ask yourself what feels right. Be careful that you project the attitude that you intend, and want to feel.

Be red carpet still

When someone is itching, scratching, shifting around, rubbing their ankle or generally looking uncomfortable, the perception is that they are *feeling* uncomfortable. So can you hold yourself still? For inspiration, think of Angelina Jolie or George Clooney posing for photos on the red carpet. (If you Google this, you'll see exactly what I mean.)

You can increase this sense of stillness by focusing particularly on two areas. First – concentrate on your head. Hold it still. Have a go right now. Give it a go while you're talking too. Second – look at your hands. Keep them still.

We tend to fidget, itch, scratch and move them about a lot when we feel nervous or uncomfortable.

By the way, you may want to especially avoid touching the face, neck, nose, ears or mouth. This body language is often associated with lying – the famous example being Bill Clinton who touched his nose twenty-six times when being grilled by the Grand Jury about Monica Lewinsky.

When you are still with your body, your head and your hands, you start to project more confidence. And when you do have to move around, make your movements slower and more deliberate.

Elbows

Elbows 'in' makes you appear passive. Elbows 'out' tends to represent strength, confidence and dominance. The further your elbows are from your body, the more confident you are perceived to be. And when you start *projecting* that confidence, you can start to *feel* it too.

This theory of occupying more space is an effective one for projecting confidence. The hands on hips pose is a good example of how holding the elbows away from the body is seen as assertive. Physically it makes you look more imposing too as you appear to be occupying more space and as such can make you feel more confident. Think of a traditional cowboy pose.

Be careful of invading the personal space of others, however, and, if you put your hands on your hips, also be careful of indicating impatience.

Feet and legs

It's said our feet (and whole body) point to where our mind wants to go. We're trying so hard to remain in control, but sometimes our feet want to go walkies! For instance, in a job interview, sitting with your feet pointing towards the door is a subconscious giveaway to the interviewer that you feel uncomfortable. This is a difficult position from which to influence somebody as your body language suggests a lack of confidence or congruence.

Joe Navarro is a non-verbal communication expert and ex-FBI agent. He has described how people 'distance themselves' as they turn the feet away but turn towards you with their torso.

The same goes for a date or any social interaction as well. Legs and feet pointing in a particular direction indicate where somebody's interest is. Pointing your feet and body towards the door might be a negative signal. It doesn't necessarily mean you want to leave, but it might send out the unspoken signal that you are feeling uncomfortable with the situation.

Pointing your legs towards the person you're communicating with signals positivity and interest.

The alpha-male handshake

Some people come in for a handshake with their palm down. Some with their palm up. And some with the palm level. So, what is the body language saying?

Well, palm down is generally seen as an 'alpha-male', dominant gesture. Palm up would be passive and submissive. Palm level and straight is a standard handshake.

You can use this knowledge of body language in three ways:

▶▶ *To establish yourself as the alpha male (or the alpha female).*

▶▶ *To concede power and authority to somebody else. Perhaps you want your boss to feel great and to let him know that you're not a threat. (It's the handshake equivalent of baring your neck.) This could also work in a job interview.*

▶▶ *In any handshake where both hands are directly upright, power is evenly shared. Also, when somebody comes in for an alpha-male handshake with the palm facing downwards, if you don't want to concede power, subtly turn their hand directly upwards to vertical as you shake.*

Putting it all together

Now have a go at putting some of this together. The purpose of this exercise is simply to notice how the change in body language makes you *feel*. If you find it helps you to feel more confident and in control, or perhaps that you have more poise, then that's great. You'll be projecting more confidence and feeling it too.

1. *Open your arms.*

2. *Smile.*

3. *Put your head up straight, horizontally and vertically.*

4. *Hold yourself 'red carpet' still.*

5. *Bring your elbows away from your body.*

6. *Point your feet and legs towards an imaginary target.*

7. *Notice how it all makes you feel.* *(1 minute)*

Of course, you may find some of these techniques work better for you than others. In which case, just do the ones that help.

Rapport

Getting rapport is the basis for great communication. People like people who are like them. And you can help that along using body language by doing what's called 'mirroring', which means acting as a mirror. If the person you are communicating with is sitting back in their chair, you sit back too. If they have their arms crossed, you do it too. But it doesn't have to be exact. If they uncross their legs you could uncross your arms a few seconds later. It only needs to be an approximation. For instance, you can mirror somebody's foot tapping with your pen, lightly moving it up and down with exactly the same motion and rhythm.

People naturally in tune with each other do this anyway. Generally speaking, people with similar views and opinions often notice their bodies act in similar ways when they are with each other. You're just giving it a helping hand and the result is more effective communication. But be subtle. Getting caught trying to force rapport is the quickest way possible of losing it. Do it carefully, and respectfully.

HINTS

■ To become more aware of your own rapport, next time you're with a very good friend, notice how you communicate non-verbally with each other. Be especially aware of any pattern of non-verbal mirroring. The more you become aware of the power of gaining rapport in this way, the more you'll find it can help you feel confident in certain situations. This is because mirroring indicates that the other person is understood, and as such is an effective way to improve your communication.

By changing your body language you can start to *look* more confident, and more importantly, start to *feel* it too. Nikki, whose story opened this chapter, found it a scary experience walking out to make big public presentations. So she subtly altered her body language both to look and feel more confident.

By using body language, you can do the same, and can start to communicate more confidently.

HOW YOU LOOK – REMINDERS

Body language is a very important part of communication. By changing your body language you can start to *look* more confident, and *feel* it too. The following body language tends to be associated with confidence:

▶▶ open arms, open body language

▶▶ smile

▶▶ head up straight

▶▶ red carpet stillness

▶▶ elbows out

▶▶ feet and legs pointing towards your audience

▶▶ the alpha-male handshake.

Also, people like people who are like them. You can often speed up this process by gaining rapport through subtle non-verbal mirroring.

CHAPTER FIVE

How you sound »

Pat was the receptionist at a radio station I worked at. When she answered the phone, callers instantly felt welcome and at ease. She had a happy voice that had a hint of a smile in it. She'd been doing the same job for thirty years, and she instinctively knew how to put callers at ease in a friendly yet confident manner. 'What a lovely person' I would think whenever I had the good fortune to speak to her on the phone.

After a while, Pat left – poached by the company up the road for her telephone skills. In her place came Heather who was much younger. Everybody liked her, but she seemed rather shy. This mainly came out in her voice. What a contrast to Pat. When she answered the phone, her voice was monotone. It was slow and hard to hear. She was hesitant when answering a question.

She sounded disinterested and lifeless. Callers would get the impression that she was being unfriendly. They would think she was trying to get them off the phone as quickly as possible, even though she wasn't.

Heather wasn't trying to be unfriendly. That was just her voice. She always spoke like that, but somehow the phone seemed to emphasise her shyness and made her sound distant.

A strong voice will help you to *appear* confident, and that in turn will help you to *feel* confident. By making a few tweaks and changes, you can start to *sound* more confident now.

Be warned though. Nobody's asking you to arrive at work tomorrow speaking with a completely different accent or style. Remember the football manager Steve McClaren? He went to coach a team in Holland and, soon after arriving, did an interview in English, but with a Dutch accent. (Worth YouTubing if you've not heard it.)

Whatever changes and tweaks you make, you are still *you*. Any improvements you make in any area have to feel right. They must fit with your personality, and your values and beliefs.

In this chapter you can learn how to be your own best coach by becoming more self-aware. Many of us are far more aware of the way we look than the way we sound. You look at yourself in the mirror far more than you listen to your voice. This means that often it is especially important to increase your voice awareness.

You can learn to have a voice that is easier to listen to, richer and more compelling. And all this is on top of the main reason for sounding good – and that is to make you *feel* confident.

In this chapter you'll find out how to:

▶▶ *listen to yourself*

▶▶ *listen to your ideal voice*

▶▶ *listen again.*

Listen to yourself

I did my first radio show in 1994. It was me and a couple of mates, messing around on student radio and having fun. At least I thought it was fun, until I went home and had a listen. It was terrible. I was terrible.

It wasn't the horrendous technical errors, the ill-advised 'sketches' or even the accidental swearing that I was unhappy about. It was my voice. I sounded very shy, and very hesitant. I kept saying er. Er. Er. Er. I didn't realise I sounded like that. I hadn't realised that I stumbled over my words so much. I could picture my fellow students laughing as they listened.

I *thought* I sounded so different.

From then on I listened to every show that I did. Regularly I would dislike what I heard, and I often still do, but I would always know how I wanted to sound and what I wanted to change. Gradually I started to sound more confident.

Now it's time for you to listen back in the same way. It's time for you to record your one-minute audio blog:

1. *Work out how you are going to record it. You can do it on most mobiles, laptops, iPods, free websites such as audioboo, and a number of iPhone apps such as Tumblr and AudioSpin where you can record and manage your blogs. Or a super-simple way to record yourself is by leaving yourself a voice message on your phone. Simply call your mobile and, because you're on it, it will go to answerphone.*

2. *Go ahead and record a one-minute audio blog. Your blog can be on any subject you like. You might tell a story, or talk about a passion of yours, or maybe even talk about your experiences in reading this book and starting to gain more confidence. (1 minute)*

3. *Listen back to your blog. How does it make you feel to listen to your voice? Do you sound confident? Consider these things:*

   Speed. *What speed do you talk at? Some people find if they slow down a little, it helps them to sound more measured and in control. That may or may not help for you. Try it and see.*

   Tone. *Do you have a rich tonality or is your voice rather monotone? What tonality would suit your perfectly confident voice? Tone can also be used to create atmosphere and tension in a story.*

Pitch. *How high or low is your voice? A lower voice is often associated with increased confidence.*

Rhythm. *Ummm. Errrr. Ahhhh. Uhhh. Rhythm is important, and lots of umming and erring breaks this rhythm. It's the verbal equivalent of fidgeting. Again, it often helps to slow your voice down.*

Volume. *Good speakers are easily heard without being too loud or shouty. Persistently being too quiet is often associated with nervousness. Good speakers also tend to vary their volume. How is your volume?*

Enunciation. *How clear and concise is each word?*

For most people, listening to their own voice is quite an uncomfortable thing to do; in fact some people really *hate* it. I think that probably makes the exercise even more valuable. Often the things that are the most difficult are the things that we need to fix the most.

Listening to ourselves tells us lots that we don't already know about how we communicate with people. Often our voice sounds different in our head to how it sounds in reality. For that reason it's really worth doing. You know how you'd like to sound, and you're getting valuable feedback from listening to yourself on how you sound at the moment. The following exercise is particularly useful for anyone who might make presentations and speeches, or anyone who works in business, sales, education, public speaking, with customers, or anyone who talks a lot on the phone.

Listen to your ideal voice

This exercise will help you to listen to your ideal voice:

▶▶ *Make sure you are somewhere quiet and shut your eyes.*

▶▶ *How would you sound if you were to be perfectly confident?*

▶▶ *What is the perfect pitch of your voice?*

▶▶ *What is the perfect tone of your voice?*

▶▶ *What speed are you talking at when you sound completely confident and you feel it too?*

▶▶ *What volume?*

▶▶ *What words and language are you using? How are you expressing yourself?*

▶▶ *Take care to really associate with the way you'd sound when you are perfectly confident. Make it even clearer, turn the volume up, and make it sound great. (1 minute)*

There are loads of characteristics that are associated with a great voice. But the aim of this chapter isn't for you to copy somebody else. It's for you to be more aware of how you sound and how you'd like to sound. That way you can make changes and improve your confident sound really quickly. This is the next step.

Listen again

Having listened to yourself speak in your ideal voice in the exercise above, record yourself again:

▶▶ *Listen back and ask yourself, how was my speed, tone, pitch, rhythm, volume and enunciation? How has this improved, and what can I do to improve this further?* (1 minute)

Nearly all the top radio presenters do this. They listen back to themselves regularly throughout their careers and are constantly thinking about potential small adjustments in pitch, tone, volume and tempo, as well as language and content.

The interesting thing about Heather, the receptionist at the radio station, was that she simply didn't realise her voice sounded so disinterested. She was a little shy, but as I mentioned before, we're often more aware of our body language than our voice. Her manager got so frustrated that he made a recording of her voice and played it back to her. This might have seemed fairly insensitive, but Heather said she was pleased that he did it. She was shocked that she sounded like that. Yes, she knew she wasn't as loud as some people, but she simply didn't realise that she sounded flat and monotone and disinterested. That certainly wasn't how she felt. This was the first step on the road for her to better tonality, a little more pace and a livelier voice. She started to *sound* more confident, and that helped her to *feel* more confident.

And so can you. If you are someone who makes presentations, keep on doing this one-minute exercise. And keep past recordings if you can – they will provide a reminder of what you can do when you need some inspiration.

TAKE CARE OF YOUR VOICE

■ It's a good idea to look after your voice. If you go to the football with your mates, scream when your team scores and then go out for some beers in a loud pub, it's no wonder you've got a hoarse voice the next day. My experience is that when my voice is hoarse, I have less control of it than I'd like, and therefore less control over the confidence that I feel and project.

■ What is the condition of your voice like? Here are a number of things that specialists suggest are potentially bad for your vocal chords:

too much tea, coffee, spicy food, alcohol, smoking, yelling and screaming.

■ And here is a list of things that experts suggest are good for repairing the quality of your voice:

drinking lots of water, being quiet, periodically inhaling steam.

HOW YOU SOUND – REMINDERS

A strong voice will help you to *appear* confident and that in turn will help you to *feel* confident. By making a few changes, you can start to *sound* more confident now.

▶▶ Listen to yourself. Record yourself talking for one minute about anything you like. Then listen back, focusing on the speed, tone, pitch, rhythm, volume and enunciation of your voice. (1 minute to record, 1 minute to listen back)

▶▶ Listen to your ideal voice. How would you sound if you were perfectly confident? Take a minute really to associate with the way your voice would sound. (1 minute)

▶▶ Listen again. Ask yourself, how have I changed? What more can I do to sound more confident and therefore feel more confident? (1 minute)

CHAPTER SIX

How you feel ▶▶

Nicole would always get very nervous around exam-time. She wouldn't sleep much the week before and would instead stay up late to cram in as many facts as possible. She would surf the internet into the early hours for extra information that might make a difference. She did long, intense Skype study sessions with friends. In the mornings, she'd notice that she felt distinctly uneasy about her looming exams – sometimes she felt quite sick. That feeling would get worse the closer it got to the day itself. She would spend the final couple of days frantically trying to remember as many last-minute details as possible, and end up in a state of near panic. Her big worry was that her mind would go completely blank during the exam. She knew it was irrational, but it was how she felt.

This year's exams were the culmination of four years of hard study. Nicole had attended all her classes, and stuck to a decent revision timetable. But when I met her, she felt the exam stress coming back again.

Sometimes, try as you might, you're just not feeling positive about a situation. Sometimes, you remember past mistakes, imagine things going wrong, beat yourself up or simply get on a downer about something. Sometimes life gets a little bit too hectic and you can't get a decent sense of perspective. Stop now and read this chapter. It will help you to instantly *feel* better – more refreshed and relaxed.

In a busy world our brains often don't have enough time to rest. There is more technology to divert us than ever before. For example, in the last twenty-four hours you might have made calls, sent texts, read and sent lots of emails, watched any number of hours of TV, listened to the radio, listened to your iPod, checked a number of different social networking sites and sent messages on them, surfed your favourite websites, read online blogs, used apps and so much more. Often you'll be doing more than one of these things at once.

Most of the time, of course, all this modern technology is great. But look again at that list. That is a phenomenal amount of information coming in. Researchers at San Diego University recently worked out that we take in information in this way on average 11.8 hours a day or about 75 per cent of the time we are awake. Different research published in the *Guardian* newspaper suggested that up to 25 per cent of men check their email and social networking sites on their phone before they even get out of bed in the morning.

This all means our brains are constantly on high alert and over time we start to do tasks more slowly and erratically. The writer and thinker Linda Stone calls this 'continuous partial attention'. She describes it as not wanting to miss anything.

And then when it comes to doing an activity like taking an exam, making a speech, going on a date, delivering a presentation or whatever else it might be, our mental to-do list can reach overflow. We're trying to deal with everyday life, and desperately trying to prepare for this event as well, not wanting to miss any scrap of information that might make a difference. Our brain gets more and more tired. We never manage to properly recharge and refresh.

Rest easy

'Rest easy' is adapted from what is known as the Betty Erickson technique. Betty Erickson was the wife of a great hypnotist called Dr Milton H Erickson, and this technique is a great way to make quick changes.

It works because you are taking yourself into a completely altered state by fully occupying the mind. You're taking yourself out of the state of 'continuous partial attention' and into a state of concentration that is so pronounced it effectively relaxes the brain.

It also works because while your conscious mind is kept fully occupied, your deep unconscious mind takes over. This is the part of your mind that really runs the show, and it acts on a little suggestion you've given it at the start.

Think of your brain as a laptop that needs a bit of a charge. You need to put some juice back in and, while you do that, 'rest easy' is magically sorting all your old files into the right order at the same time.

In the moments before you do 'rest easy', talk to yourself. Tell yourself this: 'After this minute is up, I'd like my unconscious mind to work out everything I need to feel confident and feel good.' Now you are ready to do 'rest easy':

1. Be still. Notice three things that you can see. Go slowly, concentrating on every one.

2. Notice three things that you can hear. Again, go slowly.

3. Now notice three things that you can feel or touch. For example, it might be the temperature of the air, the seat against your back, the feeling of your legs on the ground.

4. Continue this process, focusing on three things you can see, three you can hear and three you can feel. Make it different things that you notice each time.

5. Keep your focus entirely external. If you notice any thoughts popping into your head, that's quite normal – just get back to concentrating on the sights, the sounds and the feelings.

6. Keep going for a full minute. Enjoy the chance to spend a minute of quiet time. Keep your focus. (1 minute)

HINTS

■ If you're finding this challenging and the only thing you can hear is, for example, the lawnmower outside, focus on the differences in tone and volume within the lawnmower noise. Is the lawnmower slightly quieter than it was a moment ago? What different tones can you hear within the lawnmower sound? It's important that you search for three different sights/sounds/feelings every time, but the changes can be very slight.

I 'rested easy' today before I started writing this chapter.

I stopped.
I was still.
I was quiet.

For one minute my attention was in a completely different place.

After the minute was up, I approached the chapter with a renewed perspective. I actually felt like I'd had a very short nap.

So do it now. Notice the effect it has on you. Get used to it. Remember, it's OK if thoughts pop in. That's entirely normal. It's hard to focus externally so completely, and that's what makes 'rest easy' effective.

Here's how I used 'rest easy' before I wrote this chapter:

A few moments ago I asked my unconscious mind to work out everything I needed to feel good and confident, and write this chapter well. I then did the exercise for one minute.

SEE: I noticed the light brown colour of the wooden floor, the grain of the wood and the wavy ridges in it, and the square shape of the chair.

HEAR: I noticed the sound of a lorry going by, the whirr of the dishwasher and a different clunking noise inside the dishwasher.

FEEL: I noticed my chest moving up and down as I breathe, the feeling of one foot resting on the other and a relaxed feeling around my eyes.

I carried on this cycle: **SEEING** three different things; **HEARING** three different things; and **FEELING** three different things for the full minute.

Afterwards I had a calm, refreshed feeling. It felt good.

Some people do a version of this in the crucial moments when they need to feel confidence the most. The rugby player Jonny Wilkinson, for example, says he uses meditation techniques in the moments before he kicks for goal. For some people, 'rest easy' is perfect in key moments of stress – for when you want to take some of the intensity out of the situation.

However, I don't recommend it for everyone in those crucial last moments. Why? Because we often need a certain amount of adrenaline to feel and act at our best. For some people, 'rest easy' is so powerful that it takes away too much adrenaline. It chills them out too much. What works for Jonny Wilkinson may not work for you if it relaxes you too much. It's important to find what works for you. Is this a daily activity for you, or something to use in key moments of stress? The best way to find out is to give it a go in a non-critical moment and see what happens.

Millions of people worldwide do a version of 'rest easy' every day throughout their lives. And they call it many different things: meditation, visualisation, trance, relaxation, etc. If you find a method that works better for you, do that instead.

There is a famous Buddhist metaphor that compares the mind to a shaken glass of muddy water. When the glass sits still, the mud sinks to the bottom, and the water becomes clearer. These days our minds can become so overloaded

HINTS

■ An extended version of this technique can help in getting to sleep at night. Many people find their pesky internal voice starts to come out with all kinds of suggestions and thoughts at the exact moment when they are trying to get off to sleep. If you keep your attention entirely outside your body on what you can see, hear and feel, you keep your mind otherwise occupied. Give it a go next time you're struggling to sleep. (If your eyes are shut because you're ready for sleep, for the visual part just imagine three things you could see if they were open.)

with information coming in, I believe it's more important than ever to learn to harness and control the direction of our attention. And, of course, on an instant level, it makes us feel good.

In the run up to her exams, 'rest easy' really made a difference for Nicole. She started using the technique a couple of weeks before they started, and she freely admitted that she found the process quite hard at first. She said she initially found it really hard to stop thoughts popping in during the minute. But still, at the end of the minute, she often noticed that she would sit in the same position for up to another five minutes and do nothing. Which was a nice feeling, she said.

On the day of her first exam, she 'rested easy' twice in the morning before she went to the exam building. For a minute, she told herself what she wanted – confidence and calm – and then rested easy. Her friend was in the room at the same time and didn't even realise she was doing it. For a moment, Nicole was in a different place. And afterwards, she felt more relaxed and confident heading into her exam.

HOW YOU FEEL – REMINDERS

Modern life is so hectic, sometimes it's useful just to 'rest easy'. Do this to change your state and start to feel more refreshed and relaxed.

▶▶ Tell yourself, 'I'd like my unconscious mind to work out everything I need to feel confident and feel good.'

▶▶ Be still. Notice three things that you can see, three things you can hear, and three things you can feel or touch. Go slowly, concentrating on every one.

▶▶ Continue this process focusing on three things you can see, hear and feel. Take care to keep your attention external. (1 minute)

CHAPTER SEVEN

Have a laugh ▶▶

Christina was terrified about her upcoming wedding. She wanted everything to be perfect, yet she could only think about the things that might go wrong. She imagined that she'd trip over her dress as she was walking up the aisle. She worried that she wouldn't look like a 'proper bride'. She worried that the best man was totally unreliable, and might forget the ring, and that her fiancé should have asked his brother, who was much more reliable, to do it. She kept telling herself that when the question was asked, 'If any person here knows of any lawful impediment to this marriage', somebody would say yes, just to ruin the day.

She became obsessed. She thought about nothing else. Her friends called her 'Bridezilla'. She was worried about every aspect of her wedding, and as a consequence really not enjoying the build-up to one of the most significant experiences of her life.

Getting more confidence is a serious topic. But I believe one of the most effective ways to approach this important issue is by reducing its importance in our minds. The writer Simon Barnes puts it like this: 'The victory can often go to the one who wants it less: the one who can take competition in his stride, with relaxed muscles and mind.' And one of the most effective ways of getting 'relaxed muscles and mind' can be through fun and laughter – both the ability to laugh with other people and at ourselves.

These exercises are all about relaxing and lightening up a little bit.

The importance of laughter

This is a short technique for changing your emotional state, which has a significant bearing on how confident you feel.

Remember what was said in Chapter 4 about the positive stuff released in the brain when we smile. Unsurprisingly, exactly the same thing happens when we laugh. Smiling and laughing have a great effect on our physical and mental wellbeing. Scientists also say they help us to balance things up emotionally and relieve stress. So, in your quest for confidence, laughter is a key weapon.

When you do the following exercise, it'll put you more at ease, give you some perspective and make you feel better. So let's bring out that 'inner smile' that you know you've got:

1 *Pick a comedy clip that you absolutely love. Save it on your phone or your computer.*

2 *Watch it when you're feeling nervous or stressed or you are feeling unconfident.*

3 *That's it. Make yourself laugh. Release some endorphins. Feel better. Move on.* (1 minute)

If you want inspiration for a laughter hit on YouTube, search for 'Dalai Lama: Happiness, Mosquitos, and Compassion'. It's a beautiful and hilarious example of self-deprecation. Notice how watching the Dalai Lama laugh at himself makes you feel.

Even in your darkest days, if you can use the power of smiling and laughter, that will help you start to feel better on the inside. And then that'll be reflected on the outside.

Laugh with others

Jim Rohn was a respected author and speaker. He said, 'You are the average of the five people you spend the most time with.'

The theory is this: when you're around people who mope about, complain and grumble about everything in their lives, they bring you down. And when you're around happy, inspiring, fun people who laugh a lot, you feed off their energy, get inspired and feel good. (I don't take the statement too literally, however, as I believe we have something to do with the way we are too.)

Humour and laughter and good energy are contagious. Of course, people can't *always* be happy. But the more you can spend time around people who make you feel like this, the better you're likely to feel.

So, do this exercise. Write out five names. Not the five people you spend the most time with. But five people you really enjoy spending time with. You laugh. You have fun. You enjoy their company. And if they're anything like my friends, they sometimes take the mickey out of you – and laughing at yourself can be good, too.

1 ----------

2 ----------

3 ----------

4 ----------

5 ----------

(1 minute)

Now pick up the phone and talk to these people. Go and hang out with them. Go out for lunch with them. Plan a trip with them. Spend some time together. Feed off their energy and give some back. Have a laugh. You'll feel better afterwards.

Your inner animal

Now for an exercise that can help you to change and have fun at the same time.

Animals can provide great metaphors for how we want to feel, and I sometimes use them in confidence exercises. So, let's get you in touch with your inner animal. This may seem ridiculous, but be patient. You may be surprised at how well it works.

What animal characteristics might you find useful? Would you like to have the power and strength of a lion? Will it be a panther prowling quietly and confidently? Or perhaps you could be a sheep, placidly munching away on grass and watching the world go by. An eel, slippery and evasive? Or a cat slinking lightly along a rooftop? You can pick any creature and start to associate with its particular strengths and attributes. With confidence, a lot of people have told me they enjoyed the analogy of the confidence of the lion. So the first exercise below is specifically for your inner lion. If your inner animal is different, just use the second inner animal exercise.

Your inner lion

This is how to get in touch with your inner lion.

1 *Stand up.*

2 *Imagine yourself as a lion. Moving quietly, deliberately. Confident in your absolute power. Seeing the world through your lion's eyes. Feeling your strength as you pad along. As you look down on the world, you can start to appreciate the inner confidence that comes from being a creature of such power. Just imagine your strength and power.*

3 *This is ridiculous isn't it? Stick with it. Really associate with the feelings, sounds and sights of being a lion. Make it vivid and clear.*

4 *As you continue to feel, hear and see the world around you from a lion's perspective, take care to relate to the power and confidence you take from your inner lion.*
(1 minute)

Your inner animal

Now, get in touch with the inner animal of your choosing.

1 *Stand up.*

2 *Imagine yourself as your inner animal. Focusing on the way you move. The way you see the world, seeing exactly what you see through your inner animal's eyes. Now focusing on the way you hear the world, and how it feels to be your inner animal. What confidence do you feel as you see the world through your inner animal's eyes? As you look out at the world, you can start to appreciate the inner confidence that comes from being such a creature. Really associate with the sights, sounds and feelings you are experiencing as your inner animal comes out.*

3 *As you continue to see, hear and feel the world around you from your inner animal's perspective, take care to relate to the power and confidence you take from it.*
(1 minute)

Depending on how useful you find this exercise, you might want to run through it again, thinking about particular situations. Have fun with it. Intimidating situations may start to feel less intimidating. You can start to feel and act with more confidence when you have the *attitude* of your inner animal.

Christina the bride made some changes in the few weeks before her wedding. Her first change was to relax in the evenings. Instead of 'doing wedding stuff' until midnight every night, she decided to stop at nine o'clock and then sit down on the sofa and watch comedy films on DVD with her fiancé.

I then told her about the inner animal. Now I'd always done this with a traditionally 'powerful' animal such as a lion. But she insisted she wanted to get in touch with her inner swan. Perfect for a bride walking down the aisle. She loved the outward elegance of the swan, along with the fact she told me she'd always laughed at the way swans were frantically paddling under the surface. She said it reflected how she'd be feeling. She laughed as she thought about that image. That was good.

Four weeks after her wedding, we spoke again. She said the first night she'd tried to sit down and watch a DVD at 9 p.m., she found it almost impossible not to keep reaching for her computer. But when she went to sleep that night, she felt more relaxed. As the wedding grew closer, she said she'd started to lighten up a bit. She had a brilliant time on her hen do and appreciated the fun times that she'd had with her friends. And she said the moment she knew she was really enjoying her wedding was the moment the registrar asked, 'If any person here knows of any lawful impediment to this marriage'. Christina apparently looked round, holding her hand to her mouth in mock horror. It was a funny gesture that broke the tension and had all the guests in stitches.

HAVE A LAUGH – REMINDERS

▶▶ Laughter puts us at ease, reduces stress and releases 'feel good' chemicals. When you need a hit, watch a minute of your favourite comedy show. Save it on your phone so you've got it handy at all times. (1 minute)

▶▶ Hang out with the people in your life who have most laughter and joy in their lives. You'll pick up that great energy. Make a list of five happy, inspiring people you know. (1 minute) Then hang out with them. (As much as possible)

▶▶ Find your inner animal. See, hear and feel the world around you from your inner animal's perspective, taking care to relate to the power and confidence you get from your inner animal. (1 minute)

▶▶ Now think about a real-life situation where you could use the confidence of your inner animal. It might be a sporting event, seeing yourself prowling across the pitch or fairway. It might be a confrontation or situation at work, feeling and projecting a stillness and self-assured calm.

Or it might be a sales pitch, being full of energy and enthusiasm (or of course cool

and relaxed, or strong and authoritative . . . or whatever you want your inner animal to be like). (1 minute)

CHAPTER EIGHT

The sticky note plan »

I once took part in a stand-up comedy course. It was a terrifying ordeal. What could be scarier than standing in front of a big group of people and trying to be funny (when you're not)? However, as the weeks progressed it slowly became less nerve-wracking as we regularly tried out our material on the rest of the group.

One guy though, Rob, seemed to get progressively more jittery and nervous as the weeks went on. When he got up on the stage for his daily five-minute slot, he'd mumble for a couple of minutes about nothing in particular, and then he'd just dry up. Nothing. Kaput. He literally had nothing left to say. It got so bad that on one occasion he looked at his watch and sheepishly said, 'Oh, it looks as if I've finished a bit early, so I'm just going to have to taaaaalk very slowwwwwly ffffor a couppppple of minnnnnutes.'

Poor Rob was getting more and more upset and depressed by the situation. He clearly wanted to do well but it just wasn't happening for him. One day I said to him, 'How do you prepare for your slot every day?'

He looked at me miserably and said, 'Actually I don't prepare at all. I just get up there and see what happens. I always thought it was best to be spontaneous.'

You will *feel* more confident if you know in your mind how you want a particular situation to go. You'll *look* more confident and authoritative too.

A sticky note plan is a plan you can fit on a sticky note, Post-it note or any very small piece of paper. And I'll show you how something so small can make a big change to the way you look and feel. It is a to-do list for an occasion, and it will make you feel more confident every time you look at it.

What's on the sticky note depends on the specific event that you need more confidence for:

▶▶ *If you're going on a date, what are you going to talk about?*

▶▶ *If you've got a job interview, what skills are you going to tell them about?*

▶▶ *If you want to win at sport, what's your strategy?*

▶▶ *If you want to chat up someone, what's your opening line?*

▶▶ *If you have to make a speech, what exactly are you going to say?*

For example, I made a speech the other day, and had a sticky note in my back pocket during it. This is what it said:

Introduction

Story about Jim Carrey

Yale University research on writing stuff down

Write goals down

Story about Bruce Lee

Close

I looked at it about four times on the day of the speech, just to be sure in my mind what I was doing. I was ready. I had a basic frame for my speech. And if I did lose my way, I knew I had an emergency crib sheet in my back pocket. The sticky note plan is about organisation and being prepared.

Dating is another area where you could use this technique. On a date, it might be important to you to keep the conversation flowing and natural. Perhaps surprisingly, looking and feeling 'natural' tends to come easier when there's a back-up plan. This is how a person's date plan might look:

Date – conversation topics

Her trip to Spain last month

Learning Spanish? How easy?

Shared love of tennis

Any tips on my terrible forehand?

This kind of plan might sound contrived to you, but having worked in TV and radio for years, I know that nearly all the best 'ad-libs' I've seen and heard weren't actually impromptu at all, but carefully planned 'moments of spontaneity'. The sticky note plan works on exactly that principle. Here are a couple more examples:

Job interview – things to get across

> Experience of dealing with awkward clients
>
> Qualifications – especially business background
>
> Year spent working in USA
>
> Contacts across industry
>
> Ability to bring those connections to company
>
> Excitement about working with such a great team

Your sticky note plan might be a list of points you want to get across, or it might contain reminders of some of the other techniques in this book:

Meeting with intimidating client

> 'Rest easy' beforehand
>
> Pressure point anchor (see page 98)
>
> Get rapport
>
> Arms uncrossed
>
> Strong voice

We've already made the link between writing something down and getting things done (Chapter 1). As well as that,

HINT

■ Just have one sticky note plan for each specific event for which you need more confidence. By all means have a separate plan for a speech, a chat with the boss and a date. But don't turn up for a speech with multiple sticky notes hidden all over you. Have your plan, and keep to it.

on a more basic level, the sticky note plan acts as a little crib sheet you can carry with you anywhere. You can be like the naughty schoolkid who's written the answers to an exam on the back of his hand. Except this time, it's allowed.

Creating your sticky note plan

1 *Decide on five or six points you want to remember most in the specific instance when you need more confidence. It might be:*

> ▶ *a list of the techniques in this book that you find most helpful*
> ▶ *subjects of conversation*
> ▶ *five or six main points to cover in a presentation*
> ▶ *the structure of a speech*
> ▶ *whatever else works. (1 minute)*

2 *Write your strategy out in bullet-point form. You might want to write it on a piece of scrap paper first. Then write it on a sticky note. (I knew a woman who managed to squeeze 230 words on to a sticky note. While this displayed impressive tiny-writing skills, this might not be a good idea because when you get to step 4 you could confuse yourself. You don't want an essay – just a short plan. Keep it simple.)* (1 minute)

3 *Check on it every day. Stick your plan somewhere nearby and look at it often. The more you look at it, the more your sticky note plan will become second nature. Read it and remember it.* (1 minute daily)

4 *Consult your sticky note plan before you need more confidence. When it comes to the specific time you need to be confident, check your plan beforehand.* (1 minute)

I've helped people make all different kinds of sticky note plans. I knew a woman who'd failed her driving test five times on a particularly large roundabout in her local town. Understandably, this particular roundabout was making her more and more nervous, which made her driving on it progressively worse. It had got so bad the examiner had twice had to use the emergency brake. I wouldn't have passed her either.

I said to her, 'You can stop thinking about all the times it went wrong, and come up with a plan of how you're going to succeed next time.'

We came up with the idea of drawing a large map of the

dreaded roundabout. We drew cars and lorries and trucks on it coming from every conceivable angle, and she marked out a plan for each and every possible scenario. By the time we'd finished our masterpiece, she had started to feel more confident that she knew exactly how to approach the roundabout in different situations.

On the day of her sixth test she drew a smaller version of the map onto a sticky note. She put it in her bag and looked at it just beforehand. I'm happy to report that she passed, and the clockhouse roundabout in Farnborough is a safer place.

So you can do whatever you like with your sticky note plan. Get creative if you like. People use them in different ways. I know a long-distance runner who writes a plan of his race strategy, and zips it up in an inside pocket in his shorts before he sets off. Successful people have always used this technique of breaking their goals down into smaller chunks. The famous painter Van Gogh once said, 'Great things are not done by impulse, but by a series of small things brought together.'

Going back to Rob, the wannabe stand-up comic, he wasn't preparing for his performances at all. That'd be like Van Gogh picking up a brush and having absolutely no idea what he was going to paint.

I explained to him that when I did my routine, I didn't have every single joke in my head. What I did have was a basic idea of what I was going to say – the start, the middle and the end. I also had a couple of stories up my sleeve that I knew I could spin out so that I at least could survive the five minutes saying something. I told him about the sticky note plan.

At the end of the next day, it came to our five-minute comedy slot. Rob got up on the stage, and the rest of us held our breath. And – miracle – he had actually prepared something. He embarked on a very long anecdote about how he'd once lost his shoes in a bar and had to run home in his bare feet. OK, I'm going to be honest, he still wasn't funny, but he did actually manage to make it all the way through his five minutes. When Rob came off the stage (without a punchline, but it was a start), he was beaming, triumphant. He was thrilled and we were delighted for him. He came over and sat next to me and dug a dog-eared yellow sticky note from his pocket. It had just five words on it.

Hello
Introduction
Bar
Shoes
Run

It was as simple as that. Five words of reminder for when Rob got up on the stage. (Although, if he'd had six words of reminder he might have had a punchline too.)

After that, Rob started to make daily improvements and really grew in confidence. He never did give up the day job, but his experience goes to show what you can achieve with a basic plan.

CREATE YOUR STICKY NOTE PLAN – REMINDERS

▶▶ **Decide on five or six most important things to remember in the specific instance when you need more confidence.** (1 minute)

▶▶ **Write them out on a sticky note. Use bullet points. Be brief.** (1 minute)

▶▶ **Stick it somewhere you'll see it often. Read it every day. Learn it and remember it.** (1 minute daily)

▶▶ **When it comes to the specific time you need more confidence, consult your plan beforehand.** (1 minute)

▶▶ **Notice the improved confidence that comes from having a plan.**

CHAPTER NINE

Last minute ⟩⟩

Adam was nervous. Apprehensive. He could see his hand trembling slightly as he read over his notes. He could hear faint sounds of relaxed laughter coming from the next room. Well, he wasn't feeling relaxed. Oh no. He had arrived at an important sales pitch with the words of his boss ringing in his ears. 'Please don't screw up again.'

To be fair, the boss had a point. Adam had overslept for a recent meeting (the alarm clock had mysteriously turned itself off) and his company had lost the contract.

He really valued his job though, and was desperate for this meeting to go well. Now, in the moments beforehand, he could feel his heart thumping hard against his chest. If he messed this one up, he was out. And try as he might, he couldn't get that thought out of his head.

When it comes to the 'last minute' before a specific instance when you want more confidence, there's clearly a very limited amount you can do. It's too late for cramming in any more facts, or reading over reams of notes, and panicking certainly isn't going to help.

This chapter will show you how to give yourself an instant confidence hit in the moments before you need it – the 'last minute'. It uses a basic yet powerful technique to change the way you're *feeling*.

Anchoring

The technique of anchoring is something I've used many times over the years to help people with all sorts of confidence problems and fears.

Anchoring is getting the brain to summon a thought or an emotion. By using anchors you can quickly start to think positive thoughts. The idea originates from Pavlov and his experiments with dogs. Pavlov rang a bell as the animals were given food. The dogs salivated when they saw the food. Eventually Pavlov could ring the bell and they would salivate even if there was no food. It works on the principle that once you've felt a certain way in the past, you can feel like that again. It'll never take you more than a minute to change the way you're feeling.

There are three main ways that we process information coming in: visual, auditory and touch/feel. There is a technique for each sense:

▶▶ *photos (see it)*

▶▶ *music (hear it)*

▶▶ *memories (feel it).*

You can use the one you're most comfortable with or, like me, combine them all.

Photos (see it)

Remember the old-style photo collages we used to make? Well, it's time for you to get creative again. This process requires a little preparation before using at the last minute.

1 *Get a few photos together that inspire confidence. (There are some ideas for choosing photos below.)*

2 *Save them in a photo album on your phone/PDA/laptop.*

3 *Create a digital photo collage out of them, using a site such as shapecollage.com, which even has a Facebook application. It's super-easy, but if technology isn't your thing, put copies of the photos in your wallet.*

4 *Now you have one collage image. Put it on your phone/ PDA/laptop. You are ready.*

Look at it in the 'last minute' before you need confidence and inspiration. Take care to really associate with each image and the great feelings you get from it. *(1 minute, whenever you need it)*

HINTS

Here are some collage ideas:

- **Pictures of you.** Happy, confident, calm, in control, celebrating, relaxing on holiday, with friends, laughing or making someone laugh.

- **Pictures of something else.** Inspiring views, inspiring people, great scenery, things that make you laugh/feel calm/feel great.

What makes it work so well? Well – the 'anchors' that we talked about earlier already powerfully exist in some of your favourite photos. Many of my clients have found this process very inspiring and some of them save their confidence collage as the home image on their phone.

I also have my confidence collage as the screensaver image on my phone. When I look at it, I remember some fun times, some relaxing times and also some times when I've been working, and felt completely confident and in control.

Music (hear it)

Top sportspeople have been doing versions of this technique for years. Have you ever seen swimmer Michael Phelps poolside before a race? The headphones are always in and he's listening to music. It certainly works for him; he's won many Olympic gold medals and has been described as the most successful swimmer of all time.

So you're going to load up your iPod with a particularly great tune, give it even more emotional impact and then give it a blast whenever you want to feel really good.

Before you create your playlist, put some thought into what song fits the mood you want. I knew somebody who was about to make a presentation. He wanted very gentle chillout music, which he said would help him feel confident and relaxed. Likewise, there was a famous heavyweight boxer who wanted to calm down before he entered the ring, so he listened to classical Japanese music.

I also know many sportspeople who listen to something big and banging before they get out there. Michael Phelps, by the way, listens to Lil Wayne. Remember, the song has to fit the *type* of confidence you want. Everyone's different. For instance, an Olympic marksman admitted that before he won gold he listened to Whitney Houston for inspiration. So there's no limit to what you might pick (or accounting for taste).

Once you've made your choice, do the following:

1 *Create a playlist on your iPod/MP3/vinyl/cassette/CD. Call it 'The last minute'. Include your song that has great associations in the playlist.*

2 *Listen to a minute of this song now. As you listen, think of a time when you were really confident. Make it a great memory. (If you can't think of any time, think of somebody you know who is really confident, and associate it with them.)*

3 *As you listen to the song, fully associate with the memory. Remember exactly how confident you felt and take time to really make those feelings of confidence strong. Make the sounds loud and clear. Make the images vivid and bright as you see exactly what you saw. Allow yourself to really enjoy this bit. (1 minute)*

4 *When you've finished, save your playlist. Just like Michael Phelps, in the 'last minute' before you need more confidence, listen to it. (1 minute)*

Memories (feel it)

For this technique, not only do you get reminded of a great memory, you will also touch a traditional yoga pressure point to promote confidence and calm. Each pressure point has an important significance – just pick the one you like best. Remember to touch the pressure point very lightly – that's all it needs. Here's what to do:

1 *Think of a time when you felt really confident. Make it a great memory. (If you can't think of any time, that's OK. Think of somebody you know who is really confident instead.)*

2 *Fully associate with the memory (or the confident person). Take time to make those feelings of confidence really strong. Make the sounds to do with the memory perfectly clear, and louder, focusing on exactly what you could hear at the time. Make the images large in your mind.*

Remember how great it felt. Allow yourself to really enjoy this bit.

3 *As you continue to feel, hear and see that confidence, when the feeling is strongest, do one of these things:*

▶ *touch the tips of your little finger and thumb together*

▶ *touch the tips of your ring finger and thumb together*

▶ *lightly press one thumb on the bony part of your other thumb (the knuckle that connects the thumb to the hand)*

▶ *lightly touch all your fingertips from each hand together.*

4 *And at any moment afterwards when you want to feel more confident, touch again. (1 minute)*

In a funny kind of way, you are now like one of Pavlov's dogs. But this is a good thing. Because at any time when you need to feel more confident, you can touch your pressure point and you will feel it.

One of the effective things about touching these pressure points is that you can do it with any emotion, and layer all these positive feelings on top of one another. Like this:

▶▶ *Repeat the above exercise with any other emotion that would help you. For instance, you could choose relaxation, calm or strength.*

▶▶ *Think of a time when you felt this way. Make it the most powerful memory you can. Repeat the exercise, touching the same pressure point on your hand as you did before.*

▶▶ *Do it as many times as you like, as often as you like and with as many good emotions as you like.* (1 minute)

Damian approached me for help. He felt very unconfident and shy in social situations. I got him doing this: first he touched confidence onto a pressure point in exactly the same way as I've just described. He picked a time when he was in charge of a project at work and it went well.

Then I asked him, 'What else would help you to feel more confident when meeting people?'

He said, 'I'd like to feel calm and relaxed. Then I'd start to feel more confident.'

So I asked him to pick a time when he'd felt really calm in the past. He remembered a really relaxing summer's day in his garden, sitting in a deckchair and listening to the birds twittering as he soaked up the sun. He focused on the wonderful feeling of the sunlight on his skin, the warmth of the afternoon sun shining on him and his garden, and the calmness that he felt sitting there.

He noticed the beautiful sounds that the birds were making, and started to notice their clarity, tone and volume, and was able to pick out every individual note. He saw the colours, textures and greenery of his garden, and made the pictures really bright, just like the sunlight.

And he really surrounded himself in the picture and enjoyed associating with that calm that he'd felt, and was feeling.

I watched him as he lightly pressed the tip of his little finger and his thumb together. A serene smile crept across his face. He was very still, and seemed very content. Because, strange as it may seem, the brain treats a real experience and one that's vividly imagined in the same way. In other words, he was feeling the same calm that he'd felt in his garden.

Damian called me five days after our meeting. He'd just been in a social situation which had gone well. He told me he'd had his little finger and his thumb touching together the whole time, and said he'd felt more confident and calm.

The power of seeing, hearing and feeling

These three techniques are simply about using things that we can see, hear and feel to make ourselves feel differently. And they work whether we like it or not. If you don't believe me, think about what happens when you hear a song on the radio that reminds you of a great holiday. Or a song that reminds you of an ex-partner.

In the moments before Adam went into his sales pitch, he was able to use the techniques we'd recently been talking about. As he sat there, he touched his ring finger and thumb together, and thought of one of the really great pitches he'd done in the past (when he'd actually turned up on time). He thought of the work that he'd put into it and the confidence that he had in his ability to do a good job. He thought about the positive reaction he'd had. Then he looked at a recent picture of himself on holiday with his girlfriend. He saw himself relaxed, and he put himself in the picture.

He remembered how chilled out he'd been on that holiday. In this way, Adam was able to start feeling more relaxed and positive about his pitch.

LAST MINUTE – REMINDERS

▶▶ **Photos (see it). Create a collage from inspiring photos and save it on your phone. Look at it in the last minute before you need more confidence.** (1 minute)

▶▶ **Music (hear it). Work out what music best inspires feelings of confidence in you. Pick a favourite tune that already feels good. Load more emotional impact onto the song by linking it with great memories as you listen to it. Listen to it in the last minute before you need more confidence.** (1 minute)

▶▶ **Memories (feel it). Recreate a confident feeling by remembering past episodes when you felt this way. Add to this any other emotion or feeling that might also help you feel good. Activate this feeling whenever you like by lightly touching pressure points on your hand. Then do it in the moment before you need more confidence.** (1 minute)

▶▶ **Combine the collage, music and memories all at once for a great confident feeling.** (1 minute)

CHAPTER TEN

The future ▶▶

I saw Lily about improving her horse-riding confidence. Lily is quite a high-level equestrian competitor but was going through a bit of a crisis of confidence. We had a really good session, and she made some significant changes.

Two weeks later she called me to tell me she'd won a big competition. She was so excited and so pleased, and said she'd had exactly the right mixture of confidence and 'good nerves'.

A year and a half later, I saw Lily again. 'I'm still good,' she said, 'I still feel more confident and everything's going rather well. But I've got another big competition coming up soon, and I'm not nervous, but I have to admit I've forgotten some of the little things I did last time that made such a big difference.'

You are starting to *feel* and *appear* more confident. This final chapter is about building on what you've learned and making further improvements. It is essentially a diary for your confidence success stories. And in the future it may well become the most important part of the book for you.

An effective way to really excel at something is to decide exactly what works best for you. Write it down. And then come back and read it again when you need a confidence reminder.

Let's say one of the techniques in this book helps you to make major improvements in . . . giving a speech, for example. It was a significant improvement on the past. What would be the point of going to all that time and effort if the next speech you give isn't until next year – and by then you've forgotten all the things that worked best? The little things: how you prepared the day before; which visualisation technique you used; what body-language techniques and voice tonality worked; what pressure point you used to feel confident and all the other stuff you did.

Before writing this chapter I grabbed my notebook and took a look at exactly what happened when I saw Lily, and the notes I made at the time. It is impossible to remember everything, so I very briefly wrote out what happened and what went well. And then I can look at it any time for an instant reminder.

Some of the techniques in this book will inevitably work better for you than others, because everyone is different. I'm not just interested in you being confident for the next week. You have all the tools and resources you need to be perfectly confident and successful in future. So, after you have used a technique, pick up a pen and make a note of:

▶▶ *what happened*

▶▶ *what you did and how it worked*

▶▶ *how effective it was. This means giving each technique marks out of ten. This is important. Often it is hard to remember just how well something worked. If you grade it out of ten, you have tangible proof. (1 minute)*

Write it down either in this book or in the notebook you have used in previous chapters. Then you'll have a guide on how to be confident, written in your own words. It'll be your personal guide. Here are some examples of what to write:

OCCASION: Speech in front of a few people at work.

WHAT WORKS: The 'rest easy' technique. I felt tense and jittery beforehand, so I did that, and it calmed me down.

CONFIDENCE RATING OUT OF TEN: 7

OCCASION: On a date.

WHAT WORKS: I used the 'Visualise it' chapter. By seeing it all through in my mind beforehand, I felt like I knew what to expect a little more.

CONFIDENCE RATING OUT OF TEN: 8

OCCASION: Taking a flight.

WHAT WORKS: In the past I've been nervous on flights. Did 'spin and squeeze' in the moments before take-off. Felt a lot calmer. Didn't exactly love it. But was more in control.

CONFIDENCE RATING OUT OF TEN: 6

OCCASION:

WHAT WORKS:

CONFIDENCE RATING OUT OF TEN:

OCCASION:

WHAT WORKS:

CONFIDENCE RATING OUT OF TEN:

OCCASION:

WHAT WORKS:

CONFIDENCE RATING OUT OF TEN:

OCCASION:

WHAT WORKS:

CONFIDENCE RATING OUT OF TEN:

OCCASION:

WHAT WORKS:

CONFIDENCE RATING OUT OF TEN:

OCCASION:

WHAT WORKS:

CONFIDENCE RATING OUT OF TEN:

OCCASION:

WHAT WORKS:

CONFIDENCE RATING OUT OF TEN:

OCCASION:

WHAT WORKS:

CONFIDENCE RATING OUT OF TEN:

OCCASION:

WHAT WORKS:

CONFIDENCE RATING OUT OF TEN:

OCCASION:

WHAT WORKS:

CONFIDENCE RATING OUT OF TEN:

OCCASION:

WHAT WORKS:

CONFIDENCE RATING OUT OF TEN:

Confident role models

This chapter is all about building on what you've learned so far, and continuing to feel more and more confident in the future. And there is something else you can do.

Get out there, find people who are confident in the area you want more confidence, and discover how they do it. Then do it yourself. You're not copying them, but taking an aspect of their environment, behaviour, capabilities, values, beliefs or identity and applying the relevant points to your life. It can be somebody famous, or somebody well known in their field, or someone you know personally. Here is an example of what I mean:

I admire a particular comedian. He's a great live performer – funny and spontaneous. I think I could use some of that in my presentations. I study the way he talks in public. I check out videos on YouTube. I read about him. And I learn that he spends fifteen minutes before a show listening to audio notes of exactly how he will approach the show. So I make a note of it and then give it a go. It might work, in which case I'll carry on doing it. Or it might not, in which case I will ditch it, but I will have at least learned more about how a successful person does something so well.

So then I make a note of:

what happened

what worked for him

my experience of replicating it

how effective it was (marks out of ten). *(1 minute)*

Here are some examples of the kinds of thing you might note down:

PERSON STUDIED: Bill who works in my office.

WHAT WORKS FOR THEM: He always has an incredible plan when he comes to a meeting. It looks like he's spent ages on it. I asked him about it. He said he writes it out first, then types it out, then shrinks it down to one side of A4, then prints it out for the meeting. He showed me a plan.

WHAT WORKS FOR ME: I did it for the 1.30 comms meeting yesterday. It took twice as long as normal to prepare, but I really knew my stuff.

CONFIDENCE RATING OUT OF TEN: 8

PERSON STUDIED: Winston Churchill.

WHAT WORKS FOR THEM: His great speaking voice. I listened to a famous war speech. He speaks with lots of gravitas and authority. Every word comes out slowly and deliberately.

WHAT WORKS FOR ME: Not much. When I tried it people looked at me as if I was a bit odd. Speaking that slowly just didn't work, and I didn't feel more confident.

CONFIDENCE RATING OUT OF TEN: 3

PERSON STUDIED: Suzy, a friend.

WHAT WORKS FOR THEM: She always seems happy and carefree. Doesn't seem to have many worries. Always having fun.

WHAT WORKS FOR ME: In a moment of stress yesterday, I started to smile. It just felt like the situation didn't matter so much. Simple to do.

CONFIDENCE RATING OUT OF TEN: 7

PERSON STUDIED:

WHAT WORKS FOR THEM:

WHAT WORKS FOR ME:

CONFIDENCE RATING OUT OF TEN:

PERSON STUDIED:

WHAT WORKS FOR THEM:

WHAT WORKS FOR ME:

CONFIDENCE RATING OUT OF TEN:

PERSON STUDIED:
WHAT WORKS FOR THEM:

WHAT WORKS FOR ME:

CONFIDENCE RATING OUT OF TEN:

PERSON STUDIED:
WHAT WORKS FOR THEM:

WHAT WORKS FOR ME:

CONFIDENCE RATING OUT OF TEN:

PERSON STUDIED:
WHAT WORKS FOR THEM:

WHAT WORKS FOR ME:

CONFIDENCE RATING OUT OF TEN:

PERSON STUDIED:

WHAT WORKS FOR THEM:

WHAT WORKS FOR ME:

CONFIDENCE RATING OUT OF TEN:

PERSON STUDIED:

WHAT WORKS FOR THEM:

WHAT WORKS FOR ME:

CONFIDENCE RATING OUT OF TEN:

It's simple. If something works, do lots of it. If something doesn't work, do something different.

Lily had already made some positive changes since the first time we'd met. This time, she was really interested in being the best. She wanted any edge she could get over her equestrian competitors. She eventually decided to keep a 'competition diary'. In it she wrote about all the competitions she took part in, and she even put in photos of herself riding. She didn't always win – far from it. But sometimes she did.

She would write down exactly what happened and how she prepared. Then, when she was preparing for a competition, she could pick up her diary, and look through at the times where she'd been most successful. And then she would approach the competition in the same way.

THE FUTURE – REMINDERS

▶▶ Whenever something works, make a note in this book or your notebook of what works well. Write down the occasion, what worked well and rate its effectiveness out of ten. (1 minute)

▶▶ Find some other people who are confident in the area you would like to be confident. Study their environment, behaviour, capabilities, values and beliefs and decide what aspects might be useful to do yourself.

▶▶ Put it into action. See how it works. Once done, make a note in this book or your notebook of how it worked and rate its effectiveness. (1 minute)

▶▶ In the future, consult your notes in this chapter for reminders and inspiration in your own words. Because now this book on confidence is partly written by you. It is a personal guide. Do what works. (1 minute)

Acknowledgements

A huge thank you to Louisa Joyner and Davina Russell at Virgin Books for their expertise, enthusiasm and patience. I'd also like to thank James Wills, Zoe Howes, Andy Hipkiss, Kay Cooke and Dr Stephen Simpson. Without their invaluable help and assistance this book would not have been possible.

Index